Lionel Kubwimana

© 2023 Ndakunda Ikirundi
Dépôt légal : Août 2021
ISBN 978-2-492960-02-4
Imprimé à la demande par Amazon
Loi n° 49-956 du 16 juillet 1949 sur les publications destinées à la jeunesse

isahani

plate - l'assiette

ikiyiko

spoon - la cuillère

icupa

bottle - la bouteille

ikirahuri

glass – le verre

akayabu

cat - le chat

ifarasi

horse – le cheval

ifi

fish – le poisson

igikere

frog - la grenouille

ikaroti

carrot – la carotte

ivoka

avocado - l'avocat

igi

egg – l'oeuf

inanasi

pineapple – l'ananas

itomati

tomato - la tomate

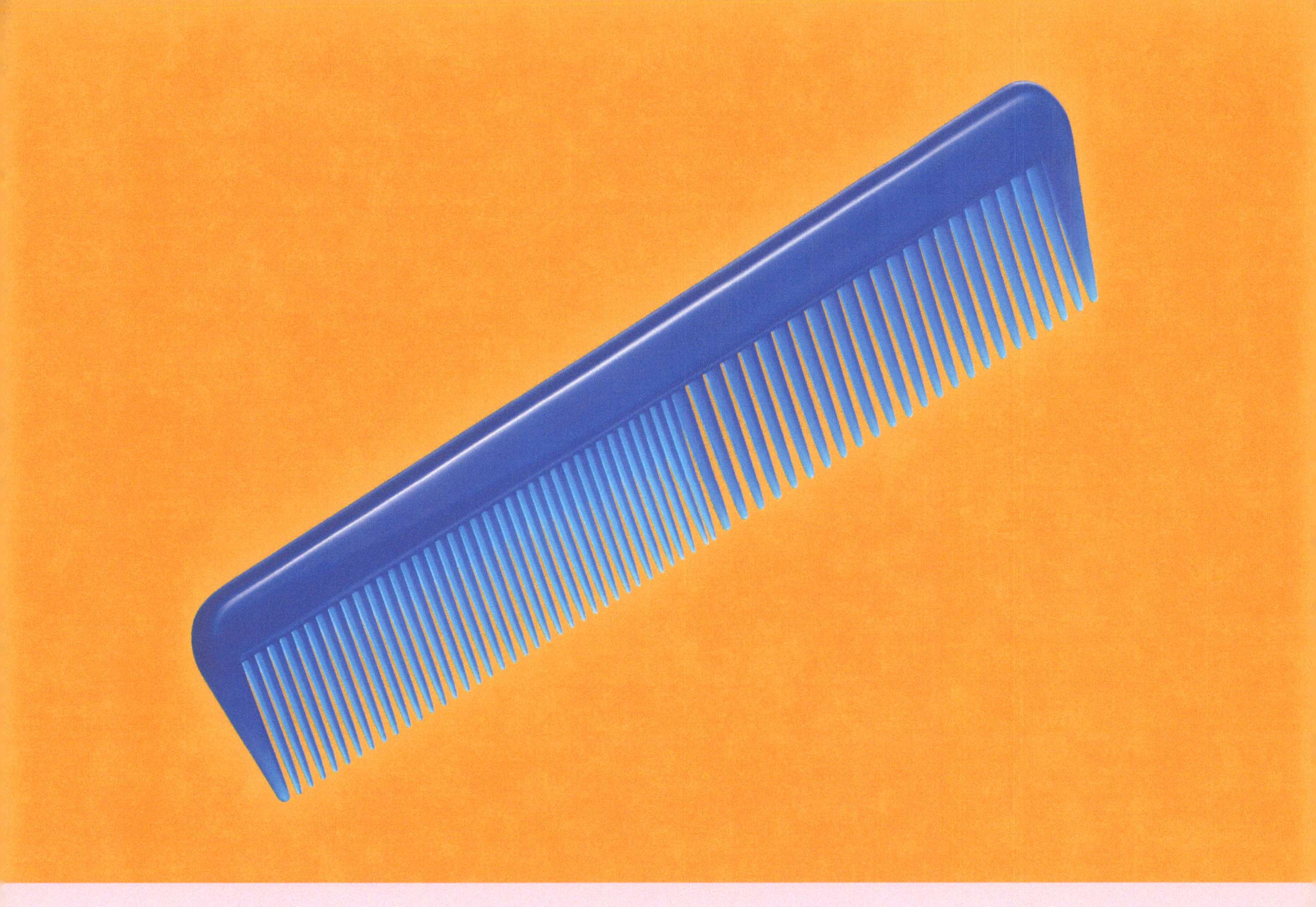

igisokozo

comb – le peigne

uburiri

bed – le lit

isabuni

soap – le savon

amarori

glasses - les lunettes

ibirato

shoes - les chaussures

imodoka

car – la voiture

itara

lamp - la lampe

igitabo

book – le livre

umutaka

umbrella – le parapluie

# igiti

tree – l'arbre

igicu

cloud – le nuage

gasuku

parrot - le perroquet

Thank you

I just wanted to thank you for purchasing this book. You are assisting my work, for which I am extremely grateful.

The best way to support me is through a review on Amazon. Your feedback assists me in better understanding your needs.
It also helps me to create and publish more books that will support the learning of Kirundi for bilingual children of all ages.

Thank you in advance for your help.

You can scan the following QR code or go to the link below to access the reviews on Amazon.

https://www.amazon.com/review/create-review?&asin=2492960021

In the same collection
Dans la même collection

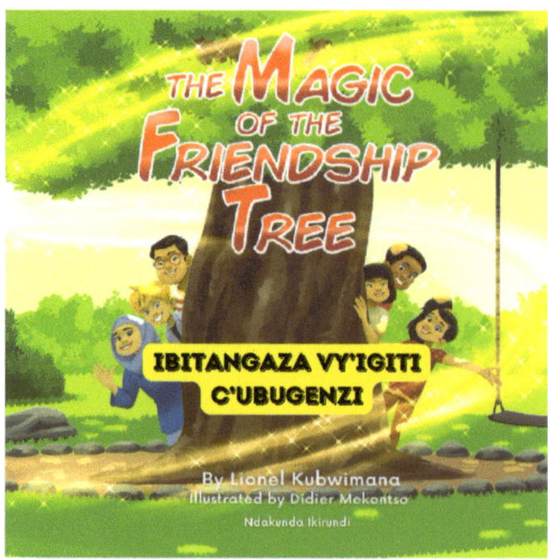

Accédez aux enregistrements audios des mots en scannant ce QR code.
Access the audio recordings of the words by scanning this QR code.